# HOW TO RAISE YOUR CHILD NOT TO BE
## A MASS MURDERER

# HOW TO RAISE YOUR CHILD NOT TO BE A MASS MURDERER

GARY CALLAHAN

*How To Raise Your Child Not To Be A Mass Murderer*
Copyright © 2020 by Gary Callahan. All rights reserved.

No part of this publication may be reproduced, stored in a retrieval system or transmitted in any way by any means, electronic, mechanical, photocopy, recording or otherwise without the prior permission of the author except as provided by USA copyright law.

The opinions expressed by the author are not necessarily those of URLink Print and Media.

1603 Capitol Ave., Suite 310 Cheyenne, Wyoming USA 82001
1-888-980-6523 | admin@urlinkpublishing.com

URLink Print and Media is committed to excellence in the publishing industry.

Book design copyright © 2020 by URLink Print and Media. All rights reserved.

Published in the United States of America

ISBN 978-1-64753-244-4 (Paperback)
ISBN 978-1-64753-245-1 (Digital)

21.02.20

# Contents

Preface ................................................................. 7

1 – Spank Your Child .......................................... 9

2 – Always Say No ............................................. 15

3 – Set Rules .................................................... 19

4 – Danger Signs .............................................. 21

5 – Let Your Child Suffer the Consequences ...... 25

6 – Peer Pressure .............................................. 27

7 – One Big Happy Family ................................ 29

Afterword ......................................................... 31

# **PREFACE**

These days, too many people wonder why bad things happen in our society. The Sandy Hook Elementary School shooting on December 14, 2012, and the Aurora Theater Shooting in Colorado on July 21, 2012, along with countless other similar events have one thing in common. No, it is not that these events were caused by guns. It was and is and will be the similarities of the shooters and their lifestyles and upbringing.

Some people may say that our way of living has changed for the better through *progressivism*. It is my opinion that we haven't progressed at all. In fact, we've regressed. The ideas of *political correctness* and *cultural progressivism* have reversed the common sense thinking that helped to make the United States of America the greatest country the world has ever known. Our children are growing up under the guise of a cultural experiment, and this experiment is failing miserably. The results are what we read about in the newspapers every day. More crime, more killings, overcrowded jails and prisons all have their roots in how we raise our children today.

We have to get back to what worked. We have to start using common sense instead of theoretical possibilities. Our children aren't born with the idea that they should make everything fair, easy, or equal. We teach them that, and that eventually leads to the child's disappointment in life, which tends to lead them to do drastic things simply because they were never taught what life is really all about.

This book is admittedly not based on a lot of facts or statistics. Instead, it is based on my sixty-three years of life on this planet, and recalling how things were and how things are now and what caused those changes. For me, it's all about common sense. I saw things that worked, and I saw things that didn't work. That is what this book is all about. I pray that you will take the time to carefully read what I have to say and seriously consider promoting this common sense approach to how one should raise their children. After all, it absolutely will determine if your child grows up to be a successful contribution to society or possibly a mass murderer.

# 1

# SPANK YOUR CHILD

Shocked? You shouldn't be. What has happened to our culture and society? It used to be that even a neighbor might have used corporal punishment on your child for doing the wrong thing. And you probably would have thanked them. Certainly, the schools would use corporal punishment if they felt it necessary. How else is a child to learn what is acceptable in our society and what is not? This teaches your child what is acceptable not only in your eyes, but in the eyes of others.

I am not promoting child abuse here. There is a difference between disciplining a child and beating a child. The problem today is that our governments have overstepped their boundaries and have forced you to believe that spanking is child abuse, all the while telling us that they know the best way to raise a child. Their way (along with Dr. Spock's way) doesn't work. Dr. Spock was one of the early pioneers on changing how we raise our children. Positive reinforcement was part of the new wave of raising children. It wasn't until later, after Dr. Spock had his own children, that he realized he may have been wrong on many issues. We must treat our children the same as we treat any other human being. If a stranger threw a rock through your car windshield, wouldn't you want him punished? Of course you would, and you can do it through our legal processes. If your child did the same thing, wouldn't you want him to know the consequences for his actions? Of course you would.

Originally, in this *positive reinforcement experiment*, the word was "never say no to your children." I hope common sense tells you that this is ridiculous. If your two-year-old is running around the house with a sharp knife in his or her hand, are you going to reinforce that behavior, or yell *no*? Will you then pick them up and love on them for fear of what might have happened, or will you spank their little behind and scold them? Think about what the child learns. I have actually seen this same thing happen with relatives. When you pick up the child and love on them saying, "Oh, you could have been hurt," you teach the child that all he has to do to get that loving reaction is pick up a knife and run around the house with it. See how easy it is to find that common sense thinking again. By picking up the child, taking the knife away, yelling no, and spanking him, he will learn that what he did results in a negative reaction from you, and he will not do it again.

This brings up another point. How often do you need to spank your child? The answer: every day if that's what it takes! Realistically, children learn at an earlier age than most people think. The excuse parents make up for their child's bad behavior is usually, "Well, he's just a baby," or "He's too young to know better." This is the easy way out of your responsibility. It has been proven that children start to learn at an age as early as two weeks old. I heard this many years ago when I first became a father. My oldest, Bryan, when he was only a few weeks old would wake up every night at a certain time (after feeding) and cry until my wife would get up and hold him and pace back and forth for an hour to get him back to sleep. Finally, one night when he started to cry, I told my wife to stay in bed, and I would take care of my son. I got up, picked him up out of his crib, and in a stern but calm voice said, "Go to sleep." I put him back in his crib, and he immediately went silent and fell asleep. My wife was amazed. Bryan was testing us. He already knew that he could get someone to pick him up and give him exactly what he wanted, the pacing back and forth. However, when I picked him up, he realized that he could not always get what he wanted. He never woke up in between feedings again.

But the question is how often do you need to spank a child? The answer is as often as it takes. Some children learn with the first spanking, some don't. But think how wonderful your life and your child's life and your family's lives will be when your child knows what he can do, and most importantly, what he can't do. You see, every punishment must be specific to the wrongdoing, and your child must understand this. When they are young, you must administer punishment as soon as you see the wrongdoing. Do not wait because the child will never know why he is being punished. As they grow, you may discover something your child has done from the school or a neighbor. At that point, you must tell your child what you know and tell them why it was wrong and then punish them for doing it. In almost all cases, the child will not repeat what he has been punished for. The key then is consistency. You cannot be one type of parent one time and a different type the next time. This simply teaches your child that they can get away with it sometimes and allows them to periodically try their luck.

You can truly tell the difference between a child whose parent drew the line and stood by it versus a parent who varied in how they handled the situation. Set the standards early. Draw the line. Do not waver. Do this for the sake of the child. I know that you want your child to succeed in life, to be somebody, and you also benefit by making your life easier and saving embarrassing moments in public.

Before closing this chapter, I will emphasize again: there is a difference between disciplining your child and child abuse. I experienced both while growing up. From being punished rightfully for doing wrong to being whipped with a chain, a switch off the tree, a broom handle, an extension cord, or whatever my stepfather could reach for doing absolutely nothing. Believe me when I tell you that I know the difference between discipline and abuse. Use common sense. That is the little voice inside of you that says, "This is what should be done." I leave you with this simple message.

"He who spares his rod hates his son, But he who loves him disciplines him promptly" (Prov. 13:24).

# 2

## ALWAYS SAY NO

Shocked again? I know it sounds drastic, unfair, mean, and hateful. But are you interested in raising your child, or buying their love and spoiling them? Perks in life are not around every corner. Your child needs to understand that things, regardless of what they are, are hard to come by. They can't just ask for something and expect it to be provided. Instead, you might reward them with wants for things that they have done right, or things they do to help you at home. As they grow, teach them how to push the envelope, to learn things that they never tried before. Start with taking the trash out, cleaning up the backyard, washing the car, etc. By the way, keeping their own space clean is not something they should be rewarded for. This would teach them that when they are on their own, they will be rewarded for having a neat room and home. Cleaning their room is mandatory and does not get rewarded.

Birthdays, Christmas, and other special occasions gives you the opportunity to surprise them with rewards just for being that obedient child. However, do not always give in to what they ask for. Remember, always say no. If you always say yes, imagine the reaction you will get when they ask for something that you cannot give them and you are forced to say no. In contrast, if you always say no, imagine the reaction you will get when you sometimes say yes. In my experience, children who get most of what they ask for are more prone to throw temper tantrums, become belligerent, hateful, and even violent when they don't get what they ask for.

This age of political correctness and social fairness is destroying families left and right, not to mention causing our children to become criminals, rapists, and murderers. Teach your child that they don't get a trophy for losing. That the most important thing in sports or any type of game is winning in accordance with the rules of the game. You must keep score. You must compete. The one who wins gets the prize. Ignoring these values will only prepare your child to lose their job, come in, in last place, and make them feel worthless. What happens after that is truly your fault. He may end up being another Adam Lanza or James Holmes. You see, once they realize that things are not always free for the taking, or things are not equal and fair for everyone (those who try and those who don't), they simply don't know how to digest that. They never experienced defeat and certainly don't understand the meaning of the word no. Cause your child to yearn for what they want and teach them the best way to achieve those wants. Handing everything to them on a silver platter makes them lazy, careless, and disengaged with life and the real world. They live in their own world where they end up wanting for nothing because it is always given to them. Make your child set goals for themselves and teach or guide them on how to obtain those goals. Prepare them for defeat. Teach them how to handle it. If you don't do this, they will handle it in a way that will most certainly hurt others and possibly you, the parent. One thing you can count on—life has disappointments. Teach this to your children.

# 3

## SET RULES

Yes, you must have rules. Where in this world are there no rules? Following rules is a way of life. As adults, we follow rules all day long. There are rules of the road, rules at work, rules in getting a loan, rules at amusement parks, and rules in your homeowners association, rules everywhere, and the most important one— the rule of law. Setting rules at home prepares your child for the world. Your child should never be able to say, "I didn't know that was wrong." Besides setting rules for what is right and what is wrong, you must set rules that will build good habits. Rules like when to go to bed, when to wake up, keeping your room clean, being at the dinner table on time, what they can and can't wear, what language is forbidden, etc. molds your children into good citizens and prepares them for life outside of your home. Rules cause organization and structure. Without rules, you have anarchy. I have seen the result of children growing up without rules, the majority of which end up not being able to find or keep a job. Some end up homeless. Many end up in prison. Forcing your child to follow rules builds character in your child. It teaches priorities.

In setting rules, make sure you have a good reason for each rule. Your children will challenge you. They will want to know why a rule exists. Be smart about the rules you set and make sure they have a solid foundation for their being. Rules must promote good behavior, discourage bad behavior, promote good habits, discourage bad habits, promote family togetherness, discourage isolation, promote responsibility, discourage irresponsibility, promote an energetic lifestyle, discourage laziness or lackadaisical attitude, and the list goes on. Do not be afraid to be the ruler of your house. Your home is not a democracy, it is a totalitarian dictatorship. If your children do not agree with how you run your home, they will have the opportunity when they are old enough to leave and be on their own. By then, the things that you taught them will be set in their minds and they will someday thank you for what you did while they were young.

# 4

# DANGER SIGNS

When should you sit down with your children and have a serious talk? First of all, I believe that parents should have family meetings with all of their children on a regular basis. In these meetings, things to discuss can range from what they do to make you proud, what they do that makes you sad, what they do to make you angry, and what you expect from them today, tomorrow, and into the future.

That being said, there will be times when you will have to talk to them, together or individually, about things they have done or unusual or unacceptable behavior. If a child becomes isolated, withdrawn, inconsiderate, irresponsible, or careless, you need to intervene. These are signs of something going very wrong in their life. It could be any one of several things or a combination of things. A bully at school might cause your child anxiety and fear of going outside. Video games can be the cause of your child withdrawing from socializing with others in your family. Drugs might be an issue with your child. Or perhaps his or her behavior is caused by the breakup of a relationship. Remember, it could be a combination of these events, or one of these events might have led to another.

If you see a change in attitude or lifestyle in your child, do not take it lightly or assume that he or she is just going through a phase. Take action. First, inspect or even investigate his or her room while they are not there. Remember, you pay for their room, so in reality, it's your room that they are using. It's always best to know more about your child that they think you know. Second, investigate their social media. If they have a computer, search for things that may give you ideas as to why they are acting different. If they have a password to get into the computer, first search for the password, and if it can't be found, ask them for the password. If they refuse, remind them that you are the one allowing them to have a computer (and you probably paid for it). If they still refuse, take the computer away. If their change in personality is severe, I would recommend taking the computer to an expert who can bypass the password and view the contents. Third, talk to your child's friends. Find out if they know of something that has happened to your child.

Once you have all the information you can gather, it's time to sit down with your child and have a very serious talk. Do not let them know what you know from your *investigation* at first. Give them the opportunity to volunteer the information. This will give you the opportunity to see if they are trying to make up excuses or simply lying to you. We all want to think that our children can do no wrong and would never lie to us, but do not let your emotions raise your child. They must know that there are consequences for their actions. Therefore, once your child has given his or her explanation or story, then you can reveal the things that you know are going on in his or her life.

# 5

# LET YOUR CHILD SUFFER THE CONSEQUENCES

One of the worst things a parent can do is to try and cover up what their child has done. Do not be an aid to their bad behavior or poor judgment. Do not become the *safety net* for them. If your child gets himself in financial trouble, how will he or she learn how to handle the situation or even avoid the situation in the future if you fix it for them? Likewise, and even worse, if your child has done something illegal, would you protect them or force them to face the consequences? How will they learn if they see that there are no consequences for their actions? You must be strong and force the right path in any instance. Again, do not let your emotions raise your child. That is not considering what is best for him or her. For instance, if your child is doing drugs or alcohol, report him or her to the authorities. Keep in mind that if you allow drugs to enter your home, then you have committed a crime. If you allow a minor to drink alcohol, then you have committed a crime. You may have to pay the consequences for failing to keep your child from breaking the law. Also, remember that you have set your own laws (rules) within your house. What have you done to punish your child for breaking those rules? There must always be consequences for their actions.

# 6

## PEER PRESSURE

The most important thing to remember about peer pressure is that *you* are raising your child, not some melee-mouthed group of degenerates from school. Where will your child learn to be an adult, from a group of friends their own age, or from you who have lived a lot longer? I'm sure that you will hear at least once something like, "But Bobby's parents let him do that!" Bobby's parents are not raising your child, you are! Your child's friends are not raising your child, you are! Do not let any outside influence, influence the inside of your home. You must always establish what is acceptable and what is not. This does not mean that the rules that you created for your five-year-old should be the same when they are seventeen. Your rules must constantly change as your child grows. If your daughter at fifteen wants to date, you can set the rule of no dating until you are seventeen. Do not give in because her friend dates and she is only fourteen. Just say, "Good for her!" and leave it at that. Peer pressure is always going to be an issue with raising your child. Just remember that the way you raise your child is in their best interest. You must get to know their friends and even their friends' parents. If you feel that the friend or their parents are not the kind of people you want your child to associate with, then limit their involvement with them or forbid them to associate with them altogether. At the same time, your child's friends must be welcome and invited into your home so you can see who they really are. Do be fooled by someone like Eddie Haskell who treats you like Mrs. Cleaver when they visit. If you don't know what that means, you need to look up Eddie Haskell and Mrs. Cleaver on the internet. Mrs. Cleaver knew who Eddie really was.

# 7

## ONE BIG HAPPY FAMILY

Well, that is what we really want. Right? It is said that a family that plays together, stays together. It is also said that a family that *prays* together, stays together. I believe it is important for both to be true. Without fun time for the whole family, your child will find his or her own source of entertainment. Likewise, if your family has the understanding of what God has intended for all of us, your child will much more appreciate why you have tried your best to raise them using the methods that you have chosen. You don't have to read a book on raising your child. You only have to follow His outline for life. God already gave you His rules, and He has embedded in your heart how to raise your children. If things get difficult or if you find that you don't know what to do, God left us a manual to follow. You need to read it. It is complete in all that we do and in all that we should be. We must realize that someday, we will stand before Him and He will judge our life. Did we follow His word to the best of our ability? Did we spread the Gospel as He commanded? The first consideration of who we spread His Gospel to would be our children. Did we make them into disciples?

I believe that if you follow the writings of this book and the writings of the Bible, then you would have raised your child in the right way, in God's way, the way it used to be, the way it was before we raised mass murders, the way it was before we overcrowded our jails and prisons, the way it was when we knew right from wrong. Do not be fooled by today's world. It seems that everyone has forgotten the past and what we have learned and what we know to be true. The truth is in His word and that will never change.

# AFTERWORD

Once again, I want to express that this book reflects my opinion as to how a child should be raised. I did not study child psychology or any other psychology courses other than that which was required in college. However, keeping in mind that the word expert is derived from the word experience, I do consider myself one who knows about raising children. I was basically the babysitter for my three younger brothers, although I could not use any disciplinary actions when they did something wrong or something stupid. But I feel that I still had a strong influence on them until I left home. I had three of my own children, and I instilled on them the same ideas as are mentioned in this book. That doesn't mean that I was perfect, far from it. I made many mistakes throughout my life as they would probably attest to. But the lessons I learned from my mistakes and from watching others make their mistakes gives me the experience necessary to become an expert (at least in my eyes).

So take the writings of this small, get to the point, no-nonsense book with an understanding that it comes from one who sees things as they used to be and how they should be again. Forget that *positive reinforcement* crap. Forget the *new* way to raise a child. Current events and the news tell us that they do not work. Do not be *politically correct* when it comes to raising your child. You don't have to spare their feelings when teaching them right from wrong. Personally, I don't believe in *political correctness* in the first place. I believe in telling it like it is. And that's what I hope I accomplished in this book.

www.ingramcontent.com/pod-product-compliance
Ingram Content Group UK Ltd.
Pitfield, Milton Keynes, MK11 3LW, UK
UKHW022217230426
12048UKWH00016BA/907